To LOVE Your Spouse

...and divorce is NOT 1

BY

CEDRIC L. WELLS

MTD Solutionz, LLC

Cover Design by Clarence "Crunch" Guice and Cedric L. Wells

Editing by Tiffani Adomey

99 WAYS TO LOVE YOUR SPOUSE...AND DIVORCE IS NOT 1
Copyright © 2014 by Cedric L. Wells
Published by MTD Solutionz, LLC
Powder Springs, GA

ISBN 978-0-692-30341-2

Printed in the United States of America

This book is dedicated to my beautiful wife, Christel, who continues to inspire me to be the best I can be in all aspects of life.

ACKNOWLEDGMENTS

First and foremost, I would like to thank God for walking with me through the entire birthing process of this book. Without Him, the content within these pages would not have been realized.

I want to thank my wife, Christel, for being my primary motivation for creating this book. You helped me understand that love is more than a word. Love is continuous action.

I would like to thank my parents, Donald and Velma Wells. Your 47+ years of marriage prove that marriages can and do last. Thank you for setting the example by navigating the ups and downs of marriage. You have set the bar for me to strive for within my marriage.

I want to thank Pastors David and Cynthia Newborne for their ongoing spiritual covering of my marriage. Their Covenant of Peace Marriage Encounter sessions have been priceless gifts to my wife and I for over 10 years and we both look forward to many more sessions in the years to come.

I would like to thank my We Honor Marriage family at my church home, Word of Faith Family Worship Cathedral. Your interactive guidance helps my marriage and many others make it through the many challenges that come up in our daily lives.

Special thanks to one of my closest friends and fellow artist, Clarence "Crunch" Guice, for the logo design.

Another special thanks to Tiffani Adomey for her editing prowess. Your keen sight and skills were key in finalizing this book.

Lastly, I want to thank all of you who are married and those who strive to be married. Thank you for embarking on the gift God gave us – to become one with Him and our spouse.

To LOVE Your Spouse

...and divorce is NOT 1

CONTENTS

INTRODUCTION

Love does not create happiness in a marriage. Showing and feeling love creates happiness in a marriage. The second sentence is the goal we should all strive for in our marriages. Unfortunately, there are so many marriages in society that are lacking in love being shown to wives and husbands. Why? It could be for a number of reasons. The worst reason would be that one spouse doesn't love the other. I hope that is not the case for anyone reading this book because there has to be a foundation of love to implement this book into your marriage. Another reason could be the lack of interest in showing love to the spouse. There may be other priorities on top of the priority list in front of the spouse, such as the job or even the children. The last potential reason I will mention explaining why the showing of love is lacking – the spouse simply does not know how to properly love his or her spouse. How is this possible? Well, the spouse may not have seen love expressed between the parents of the household while growing up as a child; primarily due to either a single parent household or the generational culture of the family.

Regardless the reason, this can change within every marriage. Think about it. Did you know how to walk when you were born? No. You had to learn. Did you immediately know how to multiply numbers as a child? No. You had to learn. If you don't know how to show love properly to your spouse, guess what? You can learn.

I wrote this book to serve as a creative recommendation tool. While I encourage you to try the many actions detailed in this book, I truly want to inspire you to think of your own ways to show love to your spouse. No two spouses are the same. Therefore, you need to figure out the ways to love your spouse that is well received and appreciated. Journalize your journey in finding those best ways.

Now is the time to do it. LEARN TO LOVE THE ONE YOU LOVE!

PHASE I

Learning To Crawl In Love

#1

way to love your spouse...

Each day ask yourself two questions...the first in the morning and the second one at night. First question (morning): How can I show my spouse that I love her/him today? Second question (evening): How did I show my spouse my love for her/him today? Asking yourself these morning and evening questions forces you to become aware of your actions towards your spouse. Your "eyes" will open if and when you realize you didn't do anything to show your spouse love throughout the day. If this occurs, then be sure to ask yourself the morning question so you can plan the ways in which you will show your love to your spouse.

FOR YOU AND YOUR SPOUSE
This daily activity will help create a loving foundation and atmosphere within your marriage and also in your home.

WISDOM NUGGET: **To love is natural. To show love takes effort.**

#2

For the newlyweds and old-weds, consistently tell each other that you will be together forever. Don't even think about the negative statistics the world presents. In an interview, I heard a professional athlete say that odds are for people who can't beat them. You need to be that couple that beats the negative odds pertaining to marriage and divorce.

FOR YOU AND YOUR SPOUSE
Consistently assuring your spouse that you will be together forever will build a lasting confidence that your marriage will endure and overcome all the trials that will arise in your marriage.

#3

way to love your spouse...

Take your spouse out on the town to a dance club. This may be needed if you have kids at home and rarely get a chance to go out dancing. Even if you're not great dancers, you can still have fun being in the excitement of the musical atmosphere together.

FOR YOU AND YOUR SPOUSE
This provides an opportunity to kick back and have some adult fun.

WISDOM NUGGET: **Incorporate fun and physical activities into your marriage life. You and your spouse must be active together to have an active marriage.**

#4

way to love your spouse...

When your spouse is feeling under the weather (sick), simply ask what can you provide to make her/him feel better. Consistently ask this question during the duration of the sickness even if your spouse consistently says (s)he doesn't need anything.

FOR YOUR SPOUSE
This questioning shows you truly care about her/his health and welfare; and confirms you are there to provide whatever is needed.

FOR YOU
This provides you with an opportunity to take care of your spouse. Fellas, since we are not born nurturers, this action takes us outside of our comfort zone. Push through the hesitation and take care of your wife...and be careful not to get yourself sick.

#5

way to love your spouse...

Draw your spouse a picture of a flower, frame it, and present it as a simple gift. If you're not an artist and don't want to attempt that, create something on the computer. Download pictures of flowers, print them out, and then add some words on the printed sheet expressing your love. Don't get caught up on how your piece of art looks...focus on the presentation to your spouse. The results should be the same no matter if the flowers were drawn or printed from a computer.

FOR YOUR SPOUSE
This shows you gave some thought and put in effort to give this gift of love.

FOR YOU
Doing this gets you to think creatively...tapping into an area of your brain that may not be used normally.

NOTE: Trying to think creatively may help you in other areas of your life that could use some creativity. This just might be the start of something new.

#6

way to love your spouse...

Every time you leave your spouse's presence, ask if (s)he needs anything. EXAMPLE: If you're going to get yourself a snack, ask your spouse if (s)he would like a snack also. You should try doing this as much as possible. This is a great action if your spouse enjoys when you do things for her/him.

FOR YOUR SPOUSE
This action simply shows you consider her/his needs and wants.

FOR YOU
This improves your area of selflessness, especially if you know you are normally mean and selfish towards your spouse. Remember, when you ask, don't ask in a condescending manner. Ask as if you truly want to provide your spouse with something.

#7

way to love your spouse...

Tell your spouse 3 separate things you did during the day. This activity alone helps to open and improve the communication within your marriage.

FOR YOUR SPOUSE

Your spouse will get a better understanding of your day. (S)he can get an idea of what may have frustrated you, as well as the things that made your day successful.

FOR YOU

This gives you the opportunity to release any stress you may have at that moment...but do so in a calm and productive manner. Doing this may not come easy because you may not want to talk about your day or you may feel your spouse doesn't want to hear about your day. Press through these concerns and just talk. It is something you both will have to get use to and grow into.

#8

way to love your spouse...

Prepare a meal with your spouse. One of the easiest meals you can do for this activity without any stress and minimized conflict is to make a couple of PB&Js (Peanut Butter & Jelly Sandwiches). One of you lay down the peanut butter and the other slap on the jelly...working as a unified team. Once ready, please sit down TOGETHER and eat the sandwiches.

FOR YOU AND YOUR SPOUSE
While this is quick and easy, there is solid interactive quality time being spent together as a couple. For the more advanced couple, go ahead and prepare a 2 or 3 course meal together - more time, more enjoyment, more love.

#9

way to love your spouse...

Support your spouse's dreams and give something that will push her/him towards fulfilling them. If your spouse wants to go back to school to obtain a better career, or wants to venture out to start a business, you should provide all the encouraging words necessary to keep your spouse moving in that direction of destiny. Another cool thing you can do is give your spouse a book pertaining to the field in which (s)he is interested.

FOR YOUR SPOUSE
Your support shows you are fully vested in her/his goals.

FOR YOU
This is an opportunity to walk along the path of success with your spouse...providing continuous support when needed.

WISDOM NUGGET: **You should always try being your spouse's biggest motivator.**

#10

way to love your spouse...

Set up an appointment with your spouse to massage her/his favorite body part of choice. This is for those that enjoy physical touch. If your spouse is not "touchy-feely", then it might be challenging at times to perform this activity. You may have to wait until all the stars align in the sky to have this take place. On the flip side, if you enjoy physical touch, this would be great if your spouse performed this act on you.

FOR YOUR SPOUSE
If your spouse loves physical touch, this may be one of the most anticipated activities that can take place other than intimate sex.

FOR YOU
This provides an opportunity for you to add pleasure to your spouse's day. You can then take pleasure in that knowledge.

#11

way to love your spouse...

Allow your spouse to make mistakes without criticizing her/him. Your spouse may forget to pay a bill or may forget to do a task you specifically asked her/him to do some time ago. Your spouse may even fail on a project. When this happens, be sure to choose your words carefully when discussing the situation.

FOR YOUR SPOUSE
Your careful approach to these situations shows you are not in the relationship to judge. You are expressing the compassion you have towards your spouse. This approach can potentially eliminate tension consuming your spouse during the situation at hand.

FOR YOU
You become the "stress reliever" based on your approach to the situation. Additionally, this just makes you a better person.

WISDOM NUGGET: **Your tongue has the power to either build a beautiful palace within your marriage or destroy it. Learn to control your tongue.**

#12

way to love your spouse...

Write your spouse a love letter. Notice I said "write". This is the key word. Take out a piece of paper and a pen, set aside some time, and proceed to hand-write your spouse a letter. You can put whatever content you want in the letter...just be sure to end the letter with "I Love You".

FOR YOUR SPOUSE
This letter will show the true love you have for her/him because of the time invested in writing the letter.

FOR YOU
This gives you the opportunity to use a skill you probably haven't used in a while.

#13

way to love your spouse...

Do an act of service for your spouse that is out of your comfort zone, and do so without your spouse asking. Ladies, try cutting the grass...and I know that is asking a lot. More than likely, your husband will come out to help you or tell you to never cut the grass again. Fellas, for those of you that don't do this already, give your wife a break by taking your daughter to her dance/ballet class that is normally flooded by moms.

FOR YOUR SPOUSE
Regardless of what is done, your spouse should appreciate the effort and time utilized in doing something outside your comfort zone.

FOR YOU
This is your opportunity to show your flexibility. Let your spouse know that no chore or activity is out of range for you to get done.

#14

way to love your spouse...

Sing a song to your spouse.

FOR YOUR SPOUSE
This may be an invaluable gift "in the eyes" of your spouse. Your singing may add some comedy to your spouse's life, depending on your skills. Regardless of your talent, your spouse should appreciate you even more because of your effort. Now this can be multiplied if you create and sing your own original song.

FOR YOU
Singing a song to your spouse allows you to be creative and maybe even silly. Have fun with this one and don't be embarrassed in doing this...it's not for you. You should be open to doing anything with and for your spouse.

#15

way to love your spouse...

Tell your spouse "I LOVE YOU" publicly, via Social Media - Facebook, Twitter, and/or Instagram. Some may think it is corny telling your spouse "I Love You" on social sites, but your spouse will more than likely soak it all in. Take the time to figure out other ways you can say, "I LOVE YOU", publicly.

FOR YOUR SPOUSE

Saying "I LOVE YOU" in this way provides a sense of pride within your marriage and it makes your spouse feel very special and loved.

FOR YOU

This is an opportunity to profess your love to your spouse and make your spouse feel special.

NOTE: We all know the saying "actions speak louder than words". While there is some truth to that, please remember that "words" do speak also. So don't discount the simplicity of saying "I LOVE YOU" to your spouse.

#16

way to love your spouse...

Fellas, I know this one may be considered old-fashioned, but it still has power. Open the car door for your wife. It's that simple, but may not be done by many.

FOR YOUR WIFE
This lets your wife know that you are a gentleman at heart and also teaches others this lost act.

FOR YOU
Many say chivalry is dead...do your part to ensure it stays alive.

NOTE: **If you have a son or daughter, it is extremely important for them to see this activity take place. Your son will know what he is required to do and your daughter will know what should be done for her.**

#17

way to love your spouse...

When your wife gets her hair done or your husband gets a haircut and/or fresh shave, compliment her/him on the look.

FOR YOUR SPOUSE
This shows your spouse you are paying physical attention to her/him on a daily basis.

FOR YOU
This helps to increase your awareness of what's going on in your spouse's life. Noticing these simple physical attributes could lead you to noticing many other changes that are occurring with your spouse.

WISDOM NUGGET: Remember, if you don't pay attention to your spouse, someone else will. As the years go by, you can unwittingly stop paying attention to the little things. Not paying attention means that you are missing out on the subtle changes that may be taking place physically, mentally, and/or spiritually with your spouse. Noticing and acknowledging these changes may be just the thing that keeps you falling in love over and over again.

#18

way to love your spouse...

While your spouse is sitting down watching one of her/his favorite shows on TV, say, "I Love You" and give your spouse a kiss on the nose.

FOR YOUR SPOUSE

Your spouse may be caught off guard by your action, however, a positive impression will be left, even if it's not visibly seen.

FOR YOU

This provides the opportunity to lay a nice kiss on your spouse that's truly unique. Guess what? Your spouse might ask for a few more.

#19

way to love your spouse...

As a couple, go to your local downtown shopping area and walk around looking at the stores and the merchandise. Be sure to choose a variety of stores that are suited for both the woman and the man.

FOR YOU AND YOUR SPOUSE
This activity provides an opportunity to get to know a little more about your spouse - to learn the likes and dislikes. Enjoy this quality time together.

#20

Fellas, if your spouse is always cleaning the house, give her a break and take over doing one of the cleaning chores. Start off doing that chore once or twice per month with a goal of increasing in frequency over time.

FOR YOUR WIFE
This shows you want to help relieve her from some of the work load in your home.

FOR YOU
This provides you with a chance to get your hands dirty in household chores. If you are lucky, maybe you both will start doing the chores together and have fun doing them.

#21

way to love your spouse...

Ladies, whenever possible, prepare a nice lunch for your husband to take to work. Make it special - no plain turkey and cheese on plain bread. Hook your husband up....put some love into the lunch.

FOR YOUR HUSBAND
Preparing that special lunch will make your husband feel appreciated and special. There's nothing like having his wife prepare something specific for him.

FOR YOU
This gives you an opportunity to serve your husband...and please understand, there is nothing wrong with serving your husband.

NOTE: Fellas, if you have great culinary skills, you can switch this around and prepare the lunch for your wife.

#22

way to love your spouse...

Surprise your spouse with something (s)he expressed (s)he would like to have done a few days ago. This is great to do because your spouse may think you don't listen.

FOR YOUR SPOUSE
This shows that you do pay attention to what is communicated and that you care enough to take action.

FOR YOU
This is an opportunity to put a smile on your spouse's face.

#23

way to love your spouse...

Read something together. It can be a book, an article from a newspaper or magazine, or even instructions about something. No matter what it is, just make sure you are doing it together. During or after the reading, have a discussion about what was read just to get an understanding of your spouse's thoughts and opinions.

FOR YOU AND YOUR SPOUSE

This should bring you intimately closer as you begin to learn more about how your spouse's mind ticks.

#24

way to love your spouse...

Take the kids out for a few hours to allow your spouse to have the house alone (mini-retreat). This is truly beneficial when you know your spouse has an important task/project to complete on a specific day.

FOR YOUR SPOUSE
An empty house would provide relief, freedom, and peace (quiet time) within the home to either relax or complete whatever task/project is at hand.

FOR YOU
A few hours with the kids is your chance to bond with them. Let your spouse have her/his way with an empty house.

#25

way to love your spouse...

Surprise your spouse by praising 3 things you absolutely love and appreciate about her/him. You can keep things spicy here. If you like your spouse's body parts, say so. If you like the way your spouse does something sexually, say so.

FOR YOUR SPOUSE
Your words will affirm the desire you have for her/him.

FOR YOU
Your words confirm to yourself just a few of the many reasons why you love your spouse.

#26

way to love your spouse...

Admit when you are wrong. This may be one of the toughest things to do for many husbands and wives. For many, admitting you are wrong may feel as though a part of you is painfully lost. I would say this is somewhat true. When you admit you are wrong, a part of you goes away....PRIDE. It is great to have pride, but the wrong type of pride ("I'm always right" type) can stifle or even degrade your relationship.

FOR YOUR SPOUSE
Admitting when you are wrong shows your pride/ego is not too big to succumb to humility.

FOR YOU
You can actually increase your pride knowing you are humble enough to admit when you are wrong.

#27

way to love your spouse...

Say a simple prayer with your spouse. Pray for whatever you need at that given time. If necessary, email or text the prayer to your spouse if (s)he is not near you. Don't hesitate.

FOR YOUR SPOUSE

This shows you want to keep your marriage spiritually secure by any means - not letting distance, job, or anything else get in the way.

FOR YOU

This not only strengthens your bond with your spouse, but prayer also strengthens your bond with God.

#28

way to love your spouse...

Take a shower with your spouse. Other than having sexual intercourse, this can be one of the most intimate ways you can spend time together. This shows true openness...being butt naked with each other. Now if either of you are shy and uncomfortable with your body, this activity may not happen immediately. One or the other may have to show true patience until the other is comfortable and willing to shower.

FOR YOU AND YOUR SPOUSE

This shows that not only do you love each other, but you are also not ashamed of each other.

#29

way to love your spouse...

Dedicate at least 30 minutes per day to be available for your spouse. This can be during any part of the day. More than likely a good time to be available is when a spouse comes home from work.

FOR YOU AND YOUR SPOUSE

This will provide an opportunity to connect with each other. Now this can be challenging if you have kids; therefore, you have to plan for this time together.

#30

way to love your spouse...

Fellas, wake up early on a Saturday morning and tell your spouse you are going to the store to get food and make breakfast for the family. Take it a step further by asking your wife specifically what she would like to have for breakfast. She should already know your limitations and therefore not request anything outside of your culinary repertoire.

FOR YOUR WIFE
This may provide her with some extra relaxation time that would be greatly appreciated.

FOR YOU
Cooking breakfast opens the door to show off your culinary skills. Do the best you can. If you have children, you get to show them that Daddy can also cook.

#31

way to love your spouse...

Ask your spouse a 2nd or 3rd tier question about her/his day. All of us can ask the trusted generic question "How was your day?" to our spouse and think we are communicating well. If and when your spouse tells you something specific about the day, take the time to ask another question specifically about what your spouse mentioned. Pry a little deeper to find out more about the situation. This will open the communication doors wider between the two of you. As stated previously, doing this may not come easy but you should press through the initial mediocre conversations until you and your spouse are actually having productive daily downloads.

FOR YOUR SPOUSE
Opening up the communication channels may provide your spouse with a needed venting session to release some stress from the day. It also shows your spouse your genuine interest in her/him.

FOR YOU
This provides you an opportunity to understand how your spouse is feeling at that moment. Your spouse might need more than a listening ear.

#32

way to love your spouse...

Love your spouse with patience and kindness. These are simple and powerful actions you should implement. If your spouse is not doing something you expect her/him to do, exude patience towards your spouse to allow her/him the opportunity to fulfill the task within her/his timeframe. Additionally, be kind in your expressions and words towards your spouse during this process. Please be aware that this can take days, months, or years. It all depends on the "something" you expect your spouse to do...i.e. fix something around the house, show affection, or show appreciation for you.

FOR YOUR SPOUSE

Your spouse should recognize your patience and kindness over time which could lead to a change in attitude/atmosphere or change the response time in the future for getting things done in a timely manner.

FOR YOU

This provides multiple opportunities to improve yourself as a person by increasing your self-control and patience. To control your emotions when things are not going your way shows great self-discipline...and you owe it all to your spouse.

#33

way to love your spouse...

Leave your spouse her/his favorite snack or candy on the car seat in the morning.

FOR YOUR SPOUSE

This is a nice surprise gift that will most definitely brighten the start of your spouse's day.

FOR YOU

You should get a nice "THANK YOU" call, email, or text from your spouse.

PHASE II

Learning To Walk In Love

#34

way to love your spouse...

Give your spouse a kiss every time you leave the house. I know many of us do this in the morning before we go to work. However, why not give your spouse a kiss before you go to the store...or before you go to the gym?

FOR YOUR SPOUSE
Kissing your spouse before each departure ensures s(he) is FEELING your love each day.

FOR YOU
This activity allows you to increase your physical contact with your spouse each day.

WISDOM NUGGET: **Kissing is an integral part of showing affection which is the way many people need to feel love. You're married...kiss your spouse!**

#35

way to love your spouse...

For your spouse's birthday, do something different for her/him each year. Of course you will always do the dinner and/or party for your spouse, but also consider going to a unique attraction or show. This is a great way to build up your spouse's anticipation each year.

FOR YOUR SPOUSE
Varying your spouse's birthday activities each year shows your spouse the effort you put into making sure each birthday is enjoyed and memorable.

FOR YOU
This causes you to think creatively about how you can make your spouse happy.

WISDOM NUGGET: Creative love helps your marriage grow.

#36

way to love your spouse...

Experience something new together for the first time at least once a year...ballet, opera, haunted house, rodeo, hockey game, etc.

FOR YOU AND YOUR SPOUSE

This gives both you and your spouse the opportunity to grow together as a couple - especially if you both enjoy the experience. Please feel free to perform this activity more than once a year. It will help increase the excitement within your marriage.

#37

way to love your spouse...

Go to your spouse, wrap your arms around your spouse, and simply hug your spouse. So that your spouse doesn't get alarmed, you can say "I love you" to eliminate any concerns coming from the sudden hold. The key is to spend sporadic intimate time together. A minute or two of this intimacy is great. You can have a quick conversation or you can simply look at each other and enjoy the moment.

FOR YOU AND YOUR SPOUSE

This provides an opportunity for the two of you to connect physically and emotionally. While spending this small amount of time embracing, you will get a sense of how your spouse is feeling at that moment in time...which may lead to a needed conversation. Just be sure to embrace the moment.

#38

way to love your spouse...

When your children's school year is in session, take a day off with your spouse and enjoy the day with each other...just the two of you. Make this day of PTO (Paid Time Off) count. Go to breakfast and lunch together...catch an early movie...go to the gym together...go to the golf or gun range together. No matter what the activity, just do it together.

FOR YOU AND YOUR SPOUSE

Playing hooky from your job and kids provide you both with an excellent opportunity to spend solid QUALITY TIME together. This act of truancy will bring you closer as a couple. Enjoy it!

#39

way to love your spouse...

Profess your love for your spouse in front of someone. This can be most effective if done within a group such as family and friends. When you depart, say "I Love You".

FOR YOUR SPOUSE
Professing your love gives your spouse a sense of pride within your marriage, and of course it will make your spouse feel very special.

FOR YOU
You become that person in the group that everyone is now looking at with envy.

#40

way to love your spouse...

Respect your spouse. My wife was once reading something online and asked me one of the questions she came across. The question was, would I prefer to be loved or respected? I thought for a few seconds and answered "Respected". My Rationale: You cannot show proper love to someone that you don't respect.

Fellas, respect your wife as a woman, as a mother, as your partner, and as your wife.

Ladies, respect your husband as a man, as a father, as the head of the family, and as your husband.

FOR YOUR SPOUSE
Your spouse will know and feel the value you have for her/him through the respect you provide.

FOR YOU
This is your opportunity to honor your spouse through your respectful words and actions.

WISDOM NUGGET: LOVE + RESPECT = COVENANT MARRIAGE

#41

way to love your spouse...

If your spouse owns a business (or side hustle), praise the business to everyone.   It doesn't matter if your spouse just started the business yesterday...tell people that your spouse is a successful entrepreneur.

FOR YOUR SPOUSE

Praising your spouse's business will provide extra motivation to continue working hard to make the business successful. This action also provides the solid support needed to make it through the tough times of owning a business.

FOR YOU

This is an opportunity to show that you are the #1 Fan of your spouse's business.

#42

way to love your spouse...

Sacrifice something you planned to do or a place you planned to go so your spouse can hang out with the girls/boys.

FOR YOUR SPOUSE

This shows your spouse you will put her/his needs ahead of your own needs.

FOR YOU

This is just another way for you to express sacrificial love to your spouse.

#43

way to love your spouse...

Take your spouse to a park to push and/or swing together on a swing set. This is great quality time being spent and could prove to be fun and romantic.

FOR YOU AND YOUR SPOUSE

This gives you both an opportunity to have fun like a kid again. Note: this can't be done effectively if you have your children with you at the park.

#44

way to love your spouse...

If your spouse is working on a late night project, stay up with your spouse to provide company for her/him if needed. Just remember you don't have to necessarily help your spouse with the work...just be awake and in the area.

FOR YOUR SPOUSE
This let's your spouse know that you will be there through not only the small tough times, but also through the heavy and rough times that may come in life.

FOR YOU
This provides you with an opportunity to show compassion for your spouse.

#45

way to love your spouse...

Be available and ready to fill in the gaps where your spouse may be lacking. If your spouse is impatient, be there to show patience when needed. A good example of this can occur when your spouse runs out of patience while dealing with your children. Additionally, if your spouse is not a good planner and you are, step in and assist with any planning activities you would normally not do.

FOR YOUR SPOUSE
This can ease the stress and anxiety that may be present during certain situations. Your availability to fill in those gaps can help your spouse overcome many challenges that come in life.

FOR YOU
This creates an opportunity for you to become a hero.

#46

way to love your spouse...

While traveling together in a car, bus, train, or plane, gently touch/caress/rub your spouse's arm, leg, neck, or head. This can add relaxation to the trip and increase the connection between the two of you.

FOR YOUR SPOUSE
For a spouse that enjoys physical touch, this is foreplay in a vehicle.

FOR YOU
You should take pleasure in knowing that you are making your spouse feel good.

#47

way to love your spouse...

Fellas, when it's "that time of the month" for your wife and it's a rough day for her, keep the kids occupied and away from her as much as possible. This might keep your wife's attitude at a tolerable level...best for you. Try to identify other things you can do to help ease your wife's situation during this time.

FOR YOUR WIFE
This will show your wife that you are considerate of what she is going through.

FOR YOU
This helps keep your ears healthy and your kids safe...and I'll leave it at that.

#48

way to love your spouse...

Pray for your spouse...face to face. Now this doesn't have to be a 5 or 10 minute long prayer. This can be a simple "grab your spouse by the hand" 20 seconds prayer that is packed with precise and impactful power.

FOR YOUR SPOUSE
This provides a level of comfort and security for your spouse knowing you are taking the time to pray for her/him.

FOR YOU
Praying for your spouse gives you the opportunity to take care of your spouse spiritually.

NOTE: **Make this a habit. It will assist in the growth of your relationship.**

#49

way to love your spouse...

Invite your spouse to take a walk with you in a park or in your neighborhood. For both of you, this is quality time spent together. If you have kids, bring them along also, but maybe not every time.

FOR YOU AND YOUR SPOUSE

This is a simple activity that takes the two of you away from most distractions...as long as you don't make the use of your smart phone an included guest during your walk. Have fun during the walk as you talk about any and everything you can think of during this time together.

#50

way to love your spouse...

Greet your spouse each morning with a "Good Morning Honey/Baby/Boo!" and a nice kiss. The spouse that is up first should be the one to perform this action since the late sleeping spouse may be a little groggy.

FOR YOUR SPOUSE

This provides your spouse with a positive atmosphere to start the day. Your morning greeting may be that spark your spouse needs to get through the day.

FOR YOU

This gives you the opportunity to create a pleasant day for your marriage and your family.

WISDOM NUGGET: You need to treat each day as a new day. Don't let what happened yesterday influence how today will be. Challenges will come up each day, but let the challenges come on their own...don't create the challenges yourself when you open your eyes. If needed, take a couple of minutes to relax in bed to create a positive mindset before you rise. If you are the second to get out of bed, you can also be the one to greet your spouse with that positive morning greeting to start the day off right. Just think about it. Do you want you or your spouse to start the day off frustrated or irritated? NO! Create a day of happiness!

#51

way to love your spouse...

Periodically, thank your spouse for saying "I DO" on your wedding day. Also express your happiness in saying "I DO".

FOR YOUR SPOUSE

Thanking your spouse for the "I DO" shows that you are still happy with your decision to marry her/him. This action should provide continuing comfort. This also shows you don't take your marriage for granted.

FOR YOU

This provides the opportunity to reassure yourself of your marital union with your spouse.

#52

way to love your spouse...

When your spouse encounters the troubling times and situations of life (loss of job, a close friend is hurt, or even a death), be there for her/him. You need to be there during this time to provide a hug or lend a listening ear. Be there so your spouse won't have to go somewhere else for that listening ear or comforting hug. Be that shoulder to cry on and simply be that friend to sit there with your spouse.

FOR YOUR SPOUSE
This act will provide comfort and strength knowing that you are there to stick it out through the thick and the thin.

FOR YOU
This will increase your compassion and will also mature the patience you have with your spouse. It will be a growth area for your marriage, bringing you closer together.

#53

way to love your spouse...

Fellas, I know many of us may not be well versed in the kitchen; however, you can still do something that your spouse will love and appreciate. Go to the store and buy the basic food items you can partially cook...meat, vegetables, rice, etc. To make it reasonable for you, throw the meat on the grill and cook that yourself. Ask your wife if she would prepare the other items.

FOR YOUR WIFE
This will show your wife that you want to put some effort into helping with dinner...planning, preparing, and then consuming. This takes a small bit of responsibility off your wife.

FOR YOU
This gives you the genuine opportunity to help your wife with dinner in any way you can. The key here is to do so without her asking you to do it.

#54

way to love your spouse...

When your spouse does something for you, show your appreciation by saying "Thank You". As married couples, we tend to take for granted some of the things our spouse does for us and the family. One example is washing and folding your clothes. You should thank your spouse each time (s)he does this. There are so many other activities that fall into this category. Evaluate your spouse's activities and give thanks.

FOR YOUR SPOUSE
This shows you are not taking your spouse's efforts for granted.

FOR YOU
This creates an awareness of the many things your spouse does for you and your family.

#55

way to love your spouse...

If and when your schedule permits, go to your spouse's job for lunch. This can either be a surprise or a quickly planned event with your spouse. If you know your spouse does not like surprises, be sure to call ahead before going...just in case. You don't want to cause more harm than good. Be creative with this activity by bringing lunch from home, or go to a cost effective restaurant to have your meal.

FOR YOUR SPOUSE
This lets your spouse know you want to hang out and spend some quality time together.

FOR YOU
This gives you an opportunity to add a little spontaneity to your day and marriage.

#56

way to love your spouse...

When you have to go on an errand, ask your spouse to go with you. Now this one can get a little tricky. CASE & POINT: One day I told my wife I needed to go across the city to pick up a package and told her she is welcome to come also. She then asked me if I wanted her to come. I told her if she wanted to. She asked again if I wanted her to come. I then realized she wanted me to acknowledge that I wanted her to go with me. In other words, she wanted me to ask her to ride with me. While the end result is the same (my wife in the car with me to pick up the package), the two delivery methods mentioned above are very different. Be sure to ask your spouse to go on the ride with you and don't say (s)he can go if they want to.

FOR YOUR SPOUSE
This shows you truly want to spend that extra time with her/him.

FOR YOU
This helps improve the way you communicate with your spouse.

#57

way to love your spouse...

Fellas, if your spouse's car is parked outside during the winter, warm her car in advance of her leaving for work. Give her the opportunity to get in a warm car that is ready to safely deal with morning traffic.

FOR YOUR WIFE
Performing this service will put a big smile on your wife's face and in her heart...knowing that her husband took the time to crank the car and put on the heater so that she will be warm as soon as she gets in the car.

FOR YOU
This is another opportunity to show your chivalry.

#58

way to love your spouse...

Express your spouse's beauty directly to her/him (looks, attitude, etc.).

FOR YOUR SPOUSE

Your expressive words show your spouse you are paying attention to her/his physical and psychological attributes. This may also provide motivation to your spouse to make that specific area of compliment even better.

FOR YOU

Doing this allows you to really see your spouse, both externally and internally. Think of it as conducting a positive evaluation of your spouse, which I'm sure you already do. Just be sure to let your spouse know the results of the evaluation.

#59

way to love your spouse...

When you are away from home on a business trip, try your best to get an earlier flight to get back home to your spouse. Once confirmed and you are on the plane or train, call to communicate the news of you coming home early. Also, express that you can't wait to see her/him.

FOR YOUR SPOUSE
This affirms to your spouse that you missed being at home and you went the extra mile to get home early.

FOR YOU
Catching the earlier flight allows you to relax in the comforts of your own home a little early and may get you some extra intimacy time with your spouse.

#60

way to love your spouse...

Pray over your spouse while (s)he is sleeping. You should specifically target areas of struggle within your spouse's life, as well as her/his wants and needs.

FOR YOUR SPOUSE
Praying over your spouse will add additional spiritual covering that may be needed to help get through life's trials.

FOR YOU
This gives you extra confidence that God will continue to watch over and protect your spouse.

#61

way to love your spouse...

When you and your spouse are standing in line at an event, airport, grocery store, or anywhere you are waiting, gently rub your spouse's back or arm.

FOR YOUR SPOUSE
Your physical touch communicates to your spouse and everyone else around you that this is the love of your life.

FOR YOU
This provides the opportunity to show your spouse affection in public. Just remember that it is a good thing to show affection both publicly and privately.

#62

way to love your spouse...

When you are away due to business or an event, email or text your spouse to say how much and why you miss her/him. Note I said "WHY" you miss your spouse. Anyone can say "I miss you", but a unique spouse will provide the details explaining why you miss your wife/husband. Be UNIQUE!

FOR YOUR SPOUSE
Letting your spouse know why (s)he is missed provides a sense of being wanted and appreciated.

FOR YOU
This provides you with an opportunity to express your feelings, especially if you normally are not an expressive person. Step out of your comfort zone and be romantic.

#63

way to love your spouse...

Be careful with this one. As a couple, point out a humorous characteristic about something or someone that makes the two of you laugh. Usually this can be done when you are out in public or out with friends. Friends are safe to use, especially if they have no rhythm when they dance.

FOR YOU AND YOUR SPOUSE
It's your intimate moment of laughter to share with your spouse. Enjoy the moment!

#64

way to love your spouse...

Create and perform a creative dance for your spouse. It doesn't matter if the dance is funny or seductive. Just be sure it's interesting.

FOR YOUR SPOUSE
This will show that you are comfortable enough with her/him to potentially make a fool of yourself.

FOR YOU
This gives you an opportunity to break out of your shell so you won't always be so uptight.

#65

way to love your spouse...

Show respect for your spouse's space. Sometimes your spouse just doesn't want to be bothered and most definitely does not want you all up under her/his personal space. Be mindful when this happens and just back off.

FOR YOUR SPOUSE
Your spouse will be grateful for your consideration.

FOR YOU
From this, you will obtain increased understanding of how your spouse "ticks".

#66

way to love your spouse...

Fellas, I know many of you open the door for your spouse whenever you both are getting in the car. That's great, but we need to step up our game. When you make it to your destination, get out of the car and go open your wife's door to let her out. Yes this will require some extra effort and may feel like a sacrifice, but isn't your wife worth it?

FOR YOUR WIFE
This act of chivalry should make your wife feel like she's the most important woman in the world.

FOR YOU
This gives you more practice at being the complete gentleman.

PHASE III

Learning To Run In Love

#67

way to love your spouse...

If you have a talent that your spouse loves, perform that talent periodically for your spouse. If you enjoy doing the talent, then do it as frequently as possible for your spouse and don't hold back.

FOR YOUR SPOUSE
Performing your talent for your spouse shows you want to please and don't mind pleasing her/him.

FOR YOU
This keeps your talent sharp and well-seasoned.

#68

way to love your spouse...

Ladies, whenever the opportunity presents itself, prepare your husband's plate to eat. Do this in the privacy of your home as well as at dinner parties, family reunions, or other public places.

FOR YOUR HUSBAND

This action shows that you don't mind serving him, and you shouldn't mind because he is your husband. It also shows that you respect him enough to do this service regardless of what the "world" may say or think.

FOR YOU

This activity may increase your humbleness and strengthen your inner spirit.

#69

way to love your spouse...

I know this one may be strange, but tuck your spouse in bed. Yes, just like you would for your son or daughter. For this not to be considered a joke, you will probably need to do this more than once or twice to show you are sincere. At the same time, do not try this every night. You will appear to be "off" in your spouse's eyes.

FOR YOUR SPOUSE
You will have to wait and see your spouse's reaction to understand how (s)he feels.

FOR YOU
Enjoy the unique moment. Have fun with it and try to make sure your spouse also has fun with the experience.

#70

way to love your spouse...

Think about something your spouse did for you over 2 weeks ago that made you feel good. Tell her/him what it was and how it made you feel (needs to be a good feeling).

FOR YOUR SPOUSE
Your communication shows that you value her/him by remembering what was done and by taking the extra step to share your feelings.

FOR YOU
This is another opportunity to reminisce on something good.

WISDOM NUGGET: Always try to think about the good times of your marriage. There will be rough times that come up, but don't let those rough times consume your mind. Let the good times control the large majority of the thoughts you have surrounding your marriage.

#71

way to love your spouse...

Gently massage your spouse's shoulders while (s)he is watching TV.

FOR YOUR SPOUSE
If your spouse loves physical touch, this will be a welcomed action and you will probably be asked to continue after you stop. If your spouse is not "touchy-feely", you may have to proceed with caution...first asking your spouse if (s)he would like a shoulder rub. Regardless of the outcome, your spouse should be appreciative of your effort to provide comfort.

FOR YOU
This is another opportunity to add relaxation to your spouse's day. Additionally, you get to have physical interaction with one another.

#72

way to love your spouse...

Ladies, this is something that many of you may think is frivo-lous in this day and time, but it means something - something to the marriage, something to the home. Reinforce your husband's position at the head of the table. This shows re-spect for your husband as head of your household. To show respect in this situation is to show love.

FOR YOUR HUSBAND
Your husband should feel the love and appreciate the estab-lished position at the table.

FOR YOU
This is a great way to honor your husband as head of your household.

#73

way to love your spouse...

If your spouse asks you to do a simple task that can easily be done by the "asking" spouse, perform the task WITHOUT asking, "Can't you do that yourself?". Your spouse probably can do the task without any issues, but (s)he may simply want to have an interaction with you - a connection. Now there may be times when your spouse does this just to get on your nerves. Be the bigger person and do the task without negative feedback to your spouse.

FOR YOUR SPOUSE
For your "sincere" spouse, your action shows that you are there to help, no matter the situation or task. For your "I'm trying to get on your nerve" spouse, your action should provide conviction that would hopefully minimize the asking of frivolous tasks.

FOR YOU
Your maturity and selflessness has an opportunity to shine.

#74

way to love your spouse...

Take time to wash your car together. It doesn't matter who does the majority of the work, just do it together.

FOR YOU AND YOUR SPOUSE

This time spent together will provide an opportunity to talk and interact. You may also get a chance to have some fun water activities together.

#75

way to love your spouse...

On a weekend day, hop in the car with your spouse (and children if you have them) and go for a nice drive around town. Go exploring different neighborhoods, or drive through the historic district in your city. Remember, it is best to do this when there will be light traffic. The last thing you want to do is go when there is traffic and end up frustrated with the situation and then each other. Midway through your exploration, find an ice cream or snow cone shop and have a treat.

FOR YOU AND YOUR SPOUSE

All of this should provide solid quality time together. The key is to make it stress free.

#76

way to love your spouse...

This activity is an exercise. Not a physical one, but a mental one. Each week, you and your spouse should select a random topic and have an in depth discussion about the topic. It can be about something you saw in a commercial, read in an article, or something you saw while driving. The key is to identify a topic you both may not know much about. You may be thinking how can you both learn if you don't know what you're talking about. With technology at the forefront, I know one of you will have a smartphone or tablet. Use that to research the topic while you are discussing it. Key point: one person should not always choose the topic. Mix it up. And remember...DON'T turn the discussion into an argument.

FOR YOU AND YOUR SPOUSE
This will give you both the opportunity to learn something together - to grow together.

#77

way to love your spouse...

Fellas, put gas in your wife's car before the "low gas" light comes on. This will require a little extra attention to the vehicle your wife is driving.

FOR YOUR WIFE

This action provides a sense of security for your wife...letting her know that you want to make sure she is not put in a situation where she can potentially run out of gas. Additionally, this saves your wife from the inconvenience of stopping at the gas station to pump gas herself.

FOR YOU

You don't have to worry about your wife getting stuck on the side of the road somewhere due to lack of gas. This also gets you accustomed to doing things for her.

#78

way to love your spouse...

Tell your spouse 3 non-physical things you appreciate about her/him as a person. You should really think about this before you tell your spouse the 3 things. The key here is to make it about your spouse and not you. Don't say, "I appreciate how you iron my clothes", or, "I appreciate when you rub my feet". Save these for later. An example of what I am saying here is, "Baby, I appreciate your kind heart", or, "I appreciate the compassion you show to others who are hurting". As I stated earlier, you really need to think about this.

FOR YOUR SPOUSE
This will affirm that your love for her/him isn't all about sex or providing a paycheck.

FOR YOU
This activity provides you with an opportunity to identify those extra reasons why you said "I DO" to your spouse.

#79

way to love your spouse...

Fellas, if your wife normally plans your date night, surprise her by scheduling the next date night for the two of you. This is increasingly special if you have children and you also arrange a babysitter.

FOR YOUR WIFE
Planning the date shows your wife you want to spend some time with her.

FOR YOU
This provides an opportunity to give your wife a break from the planning duties.

WISDOM NUGGET: **A "date night" at least once a month does your marriage good. It's your chance to rejuvenate the romantic fire in your marriage.**

#80

way to love your spouse...

Understand the flow of the family finances and be a partner in establishing and monitoring the family's financial structure. This helps to strengthen the marriage bond...especially if the two of you are in agreement and are adhering to what was established.

FOR YOU AND YOUR SPOUSE
While this isn't a direct showing of love towards each other, it does show the unity between the two of you. It helps to preserve your love for each other.

#81

way to love your spouse...

Ask your spouse to wear something different to bed (not the normal t-shirt and shorts, or the "all the time" night-gown). Express your desire to see her/him in something nice and unique.

FOR YOUR SPOUSE

This should make your spouse feel desired and wanted - especially if you back it up with generous praise of how (s)he looks.

FOR YOU

You get to look at your spouse in something different for a change during bedtime. It may spark some much needed excitement within the intimacy arena. Have fun with this one.

#82

way to love your spouse...

Email or text your spouse an original prayer that focuses on the growth of your marriage.

FOR YOUR SPOUSE

This shows you are deeply vested in your marriage. This also reminds your spouse that you are nurturing your personal relationship with God.

FOR YOU

Believe it or not, this action actually helps you mature and deepen your relationship with God. But first, make sure you do have a sincere connection with Him to ensure you are not just doing this to impress your spouse.

#83

way to love your spouse...

Fellas, on your next fun outing with your spouse, give her a piggy-back ride. Now I must put this disclaimer out there...do not do this if you have physical concerns or constraints (ie. don't do this if you know your knees are bad). Just remember you won't be carrying a 5 year old child on your back. This will be a grown woman.

FOR YOU AND YOUR SPOUSE

The overall purpose is to have some fun while spending time with each other. At the same time, you get to show the world the fun you are having as a married couple. The world needs to see this interaction in marriages.

#84

way to love your spouse...

If your spouse loves coffee, treat your spouse by taking her/him to a latte shop of choice. If you have kids, it's cool to bring them along as well. Coffee shops normally have kid-friendly drinks they can sip on such as hot chocolate or milk.

FOR YOUR SPOUSE
This will be a well-received token of love. Plus, your spouse gets a little quality time while enjoying the drinks and atmosphere with you.

FOR YOU
Your "brownie points" count should go up.

#85

way to love your spouse...

Dress up in a stupid/crazy/funny outfit for your spouse and act out a funny scene related to your outfit. This will keep fun and excitement in your relationship. Try to dress in something out of your character. Fellas, put together your best Rambo impersonation. Ladies, now is the time to become Mrs. Strawberry Shortcake or any other character.

FOR YOUR SPOUSE
Performing this activity shows your spouse you have a sense of humor...even if you're not known to be funny. This could be an area of growth for your relationship...laughter.

FOR YOU
This could be a stress reliever for you - a way to release tension due to work, financial issues, marital ups and downs, or just life itself.

#86

way to love your spouse...

Ask for and consider your spouse's opinion regarding key family decisions. Take this a step further and also include your spouse's opinion in personal decisions you are looking to make.

FOR YOUR SPOUSE
This shows your spouse the value you have for her/his opinion in your decision making process - providing a feeling of worth.

FOR YOU
A different perspective may be provided that can give you better insight into your situation to make a more informed decision.

#87

way to love your spouse...

Work to enhance something about yourself that you know your spouse would like to see improved. This can be physical or psychological. If your spouse has been concerned about your health, make an effort to be aware of what you are eating and maybe look into increasing your physical activity to become healthier. If your spouse would like to see your attitude or behavior improve in certain areas, make the effort to adjust it. However, we all know this is easier said than done.

FOR YOUR SPOUSE
Your efforts will say a lot when (s)he sees you making changes in areas previously discussed with you. If you don't know what your spouse would like to see changed about you, ASK.

FOR YOU
This provides you with an opportunity to improve yourself. Please know that your spouse should have your best interest at heart. Trust your spouse's recommended changes and go for it.

#88

way to love your spouse...

Pamper your spouse in an area they are not   expect-
ing. Prime Example: My wife offered to give me a pedicure
once...and she hates my feet. Find that sacrificial area to
pamper your spouse. If not the feet, it could be washing or
scratching your spouse's hair/head. Hopefully you can identify something you don't mind doing so that it won't be a
strain for you.

FOR YOUR SPOUSE
This will simply be a pleasurable delight for your spouse.

FOR YOU
Pampering your spouse provides you with an opportunity to
be a servant for your spouse.

#89

way to love your spouse...

When your spouse comes home from work, put down whatever you are doing so that you can greet your spouse in a welcoming and inviting manner. Think about how your small kids (if you have them) greet you when they see you. You probably get a big hug and kiss from the little ones, and a big smile on top of that. Think about that feeling. Now consider how your spouse will feel when these same actions come from you when (s)he gets home from work. Better yet, consider how you would feel if your spouse did it for you.

FOR YOU AND YOUR SPOUSE

This activity will help brighten the atmosphere within the house and lead to a great evening. It makes home the most welcoming place to be.

#90

way to love your spouse...

Ladies, while lying in bed with your husband, position yourself in his arms and rest your hand on his chest or abdominal area and gently rub the area in a relaxing manner.

FOR YOUR HUSBAND
This provides comfort and relaxation for your husband, especially if he enjoys your touch.

FOR YOU
Being in your spouse's arms should provide a feeling of security, but only if you fully release your body into his arms. Enjoy the cuddling!

#91

way to love your spouse...

When you have a bad day at work, don't come home angry at everyone in your household, including your spouse. Did they cause you to have a bad day at work? Probably not. It would be best to leave the frustrations of work at work. However, if that is not possible, simply tell your spouse that you had a bad day so (s)he is aware and can therefore be considerate of your current emotional state.

FOR YOU AND YOUR SPOUSE

Leaving your work frustrations at work will tremendously help keep peace at home and in your marriage. Also, don't forget to talk to your spouse about your day. Getting it off your chest can help relieve the frustration.

#92

way to love your spouse...

Now this item would automatically prompt the word "mannish" for boys and "fast" for girls. These are old school terms some of you may not have heard of. "Feel up" your spouse as you pass by. For those of you that still don't understand, as you walk past your spouse, rub, pat, or grab your spouse's butt (or other body parts that are acceptable). Make it quick and keep moving...just in case.

FOR YOUR SPOUSE
This will show your spouse the desire you have for her/him.

FOR YOU
It's an opportunity to interact in a fun and exciting manner.

#93

way to love your spouse...

Slow dance with your spouse. Grab your smartphone or tablet or a good old faithful radio and put on some slow dance music so you both can join in rhythm together. This is something you can do sporadically while at home or when not at home (for the daring couples that would break out dancing in public).

FOR YOU AND YOUR SPOUSE

This should add some unexpected excitement, some quality time, some close body contact, and intimacy to your relationship. Do this as often as time permits.

#94

way to love your spouse...

Ladies, build up your husband's confidence as a husband. That's right, give your husband an ego! This can only be done by praising him more than talking negatively about him.

FOR YOUR HUSBAND
Your words will provide motivation for him to want to be the best.

FOR YOU
As his wife, you sit back and reap the benefits of your husband striving to be the best husband possible. Just remember, this is not an overnight process. Be patient and enjoy the journey.

WISDOM NUGGET: **The tongue within your mouth is a powerful weapon. If used improperly, it can destroy your husband and eventually your marriage. With proper use, you can speak greatness into your husband and can help him grow into the husband he is meant to be for you and your family.**

#95

way to love your spouse...

When something exciting happens to you in the middle of the day, call or text your spouse to let her/him know about it.

FOR YOUR SPOUSE
This shows your spouse you thought about her/him first before anyone else (best friend, mom, dad, brother, or sister). This says, "Spouse, you are my 1st PRIORITY".

FOR YOU
It's an opportunity to share your enjoyment with your spouse allowing you to grow closer by "enjoying exciting experiences together".

WISDOM NUGGET: **Keep your spouse your Best Friend.**

#96

way to love your spouse...

Be as honest as possible about your feelings with your spouse. "Honest as possible" means you may have to tone down the delivery of how you are feeling, especially if you are angry with your spouse. As stated previously, your tongue can either build up or destroy your relationship. Use wisdom to figure out the best way to communicate when you are upset. For other instances, let your spouse know how you feel and why you feel the way you do. These instances can be as varied as an altercation with a co-worker to the thoughts and feelings of an awkward dream.

FOR YOUR SPOUSE
This shows that you love enough to open up and truly expose yourself - without any filters. The careful delivery of your feelings will also show your growth in the area of communication.

FOR YOU
Being honest about your feelings allows you to be your "true self" to your spouse. This should strengthen your marriage as you grow closer through the understanding of each other's feelings.

#97

way to love your spouse...

Whenever your spouse cooks dinner, let your spouse know specifically what you enjoyed about the meal. If the chicken was great, say so. If the waffles were great, say so.

FOR YOUR SPOUSE
Your words will let your spouse know the cooking efforts that were made are greatly appreciated.

FOR YOU
Giving praise to the efforts that were done in the kitchen provides an opportunity to be nice and loving to your spouse.

#98

way to love your spouse...

This may be the toughest thing to do when it comes to show-ing your spouse love, but I have no doubt it can be one of the most impactful. Stop doing, get rid of, and eliminate whatev-er activity, attitude, or addiction that may be affecting your spouse and your marriage. This can range from infidelity to physical or verbal abuse, to irresponsible spending, or even habitual negative attitudes. This is a gut check item because this requires you to look at what specific things you are doing to contribute to a negative impact on your marriage.

FOR YOUR SPOUSE
To attempt to do a 180 degree turnaround in this area is a great showing of love, and it lets your spouse know that you want your marriage to last. Your commitment to change also shows true selflessness.

FOR YOU
This provides the opportunity to become a better wife/husband - an opportunity to start a new path that will heal and strengthen your marriage. This item is not easy, but it is worth the effort.

#99

way to love your spouse...

Lastly, ask your spouse directly how (s)he needs to be shown love. This is the simplest way to understand your spouse because it's coming straight from your spouse's mouth.

FOR YOUR SPOUSE
This shows your commitment to building and growing your marital relationship.

FOR YOU
This is your opportunity to get the answers to the test many couples tend to fail...the "Showing Love To My Spouse Test".

CLOSING WISDOM NUGGET: Don't let pride or fear of what may be said deter you from asking this intimate question. Don't be ignorant or naive in thinking you are God's gift to your spouse and that's enough to stay married. Marriage is a gift from God, but it must be nurtured with love so that it will continue to grow. Just remember, when you don't know something, you have to ask. Then you can begin the process of learning how best to love your spouse.

There are many ways to love your spouse. Find the ways that fit for your spouse and know that divorce is not one of them. Enjoy the creative journey of marriage!

Share your thoughts at

www.cedricwellsbooks.com

or

99waysbooks@gmail.com

ABOUT THE AUTHOR

Cedric Wells is a husband (to Christel) and father (to William, Bryce, and Addison) dedicated to ensuring his family is loved and protected. In addition to being a family man, Cedric is also an artist who has produced works that have been showcased in galleries, at Fortune 500 companies, and at private shows and national conventions (www.cedricwells.com).

Cedric is originally from Itta Bena, MS, attended Southern University A&M College, served as a United States Army Officer for several years overseas, and now resides in the Atlanta, GA Metro Area.

Married for 10+ years, Cedric is passionate about seeing and helping marriages last. With the help of his wife, the Godly couple strives to be role models for other couples to follow in their marriage journey. Cedric has served as a resident blogger on the website, Black Love Forum. He also contributed as a guest blogger on the highly acclaimed website, Black and Married with Kids.

Cedric continues to seek knowledge and wisdom on ways to make his marriage along with other marriages strong and healthy. It's a journey that he enjoys and looks forward to what lies ahead for his family and marriage.